FUNNY JOKES FOR 12 YEAR OLD KIDS

100+ Crazy Jokes That Will Make You Laugh Out Loud!

Cooper the Pooper

© **Copyright 2021 Cooper the Pooper - All rights reserved.**

The content contained within this book may not be reproduced, duplicated or transmitted without direct written permission from the author or the publisher.

Under no circumstances will any blame or legal responsibility be held against the publisher, or author, for any damages, reparation or monetary loss due to the information contained within this book, either directly or indirectly.

Legal Notice:

This book is copyright protected. It is only for personal use. You cannot amend, distribute, sell, use, quote or paraphrase any part, or the content within this book, without the consent of the author or publisher.

Disclaimer Notice:

Please note the information contained within this document is for educational and entertainment purposes only. All effort has been executed to present accurate, up to date, reliable, complete information. No warranties of any kind are declared or implied. Readers acknowledge that the author is not engaged in the rendering of legal, financial, medical or professional advice. The content within this book has been derived from various sources. Please consult a licensed professional before attempting any techniques outlined in this book.

By reading this document, the reader agrees that under no circumstances is the author responsible for any losses, direct or indirect, that are incurred as a result of the use of the information contained within this document, including, but not limited to, errors, omissions or inaccuracies.

TABLE OF CONTENTS

Table of Contents 3

Introduction 4

Chapter 1: Funny Jokes 6

Chapter 2: Crazy Jokes 18

Chapter 3: Laugh-out-Loud Jokes 30

Chapter 4: Knock-Knock Jokes 42

Chapter 5: Bonus Jokes 54

Final Words 66

INTRODUCTION

Honestly, is there anything better than telling a good joke?

Watching the faces of your friends break into huge smiles? Seeing them start laughing uncontrollably? Spotting them gasping for air because they are laughing so hard?

I am pretty sure there is nothing better.

In fact, this was why I decided to write this book in the first place.

See, I have always loved telling jokes. Even when I was a little puppy, I would spend all my time searching for funny jokes so I could share them with my friends and family. Hilarious jokes that would have them laughing non-stop as soon as they heard the punchline.

But I quickly realized that the world is full of really bad jokes — and let's face it — there is nothing worse than hearing a bad joke.

Which is where this book enters the discussion.

I spent years searching the world for the funniest jokes

on the planet so I could put them into a fantastic book of jokes. A book of jokes that has no bad jokes.

And now you have the end result. A book that contains the best jokes in the world, designed especially for 12-year-old kids. A book where every joke will crack and smile and create a laugh.

But there is more to it than that.

See, the jokes in this book get better the more times you share them. Which means that you should write down your favorites so you can tell them to your friends and family time and time again.

So, what are you waiting for? Start reading the funniest jokes for 12-year-old kids!

Where do you buy medicine for pigs and chickens?

- **At the farmacy.**

Who keeps the ocean clean?

- **The mermaid.**

3

Why did the airplane get sent to his room?

- **It had a bad altitude.**

4

What's a recycling bin's favorite reading?

- **Litter-ature.**

5

What kind of building weighs the least?

- **A lighthouse.**

6

How do billboards talk?

- **In sign language.**

What did the ghost say to the other ghost?

- **Do you believe in humans?**

Why didn't the skeleton go to the party?

- **He had no body to go with!**

9

How did the computer catch a cold?

- It left its Windows open!

10

How did you know that doctor was fake?

- She had good handwriting.

Why do magicians do so well in school?

- **They're good at trick questions.**

How did the beauty school student do on her manicure test?

- **She nailed it.**

13

Why is History the fruitiest school subject?

- **Because it is full of dates!**

14

How do you get straight A's?

- **By using a ruler!**

Why did the student eat his homework?

- Because the teacher told him it was a piece of cake.

Why are teddy bears never hungry?

- Because they are always stuffed.

17

Where do pencils live?

- **Pencil-vania.**

18

How do you cut an ocean in half?

- **With a sea-saw.**

19

Why did the policeman stay in bed?

- **He was undercover.**

20

What is the best day to cook?

- **Fry-day.**

What did the cow say to NASA?

- I want to go to the Milky Way!

Where do you find the tallest building?

- In the library.
It has a thousand stories!

What do you get when you cross a pig and a tree?

- **A pork-upine.**

How do you make a hot dog stand?

- **Take away his chair.**

Why do fish live in salt water?

- Because pepper makes them sneeze!

Why do seagulls fly over the sea?

- If they flew over the bay, they would be bagels.

5

Why isn't there a clock in the library?

- Because it tocks too much.

6

Why did the woman become an archaeologist?

- Because her career was in ruins.

What is an elevator's favorite exercise?

- **Push-ups.**

What happened to the man who crossed a witch with a clock?

- **He got a brooms-tick!**

9

Why do the French like to eat snails?

- Because they don't like fast food.

10

What kind of candy is never on time?

- Choco-late.

Why was the apple so lonely?

- Because the banana split.

What do you call a bird on an airplane?

- Lazy.

13

What's scarier than a monster?

- A momster.

14

What do you ask your sister if she's crying?

- Are you having a cri-sis?

Why can't Cinderella play soccer?

- Because she's always running away from the ball.

Why do scissors always win a race?

- Because they take a shortcut!

17

What do you call it when the butcher gives you the wrong order?

- A mis-steak.

18

What are baby snowmen called?

- Chill-dren.

19

Where do cars go to swim?

- At a carpool!

20

How can you burn 1,000 calories fast?

- Don't open the door for the pizza guy.

21

What did you get for Christmas?

- **Fat! I got fat!**

22

Why did the math book go to the therapist?

- **It had too many problems!**

CHAPTER 3
LAUGH-OUT-LOUD JOKES

1

Where does a turtle go when it's raining?

• **A shell-ter!**

2

What do you call a naked bear?

• **A bare.**

3

Have you heard of the elephant that doesn't really matter?

- It's irr-elephant.

4

What was the skeleton looking for at the mall?

- The Body Shop.

5

Why did Santa's elves go to school?

- **To learn the elf-abet.**

6

Why was the airplane ill?

- **He had the flew!**

7

Why did the cannon have trouble finding work?

- **Because it kept getting fired.**

8

Why didn't the telephone pass the eighth grade?

- **It wasn't a smart phone.**

9

Why did they bury the battery?

- **Because it was dead.**

10

Where do TVs go for vacation?

- **Remote islands.**

11

What do you call a funny mountain?

- **Hill-arious!**

12

Why do you go to bed every night?

- **Because the bed won't come to me.**

13

Why was the burglar so sensitive?

- **He takes things personally.**

14

Where do liars learn to lie?

- **At the lie-brary.**

What did you get for your birthday?

- Older.

Why did the blind man fall into that well?

- Because he couldn't see that well.

What do you call an old toothless bear?

- A gummy bear!

Where would an elephant store its belongings?

- In its trunk.

19

How did the telephone operator propose to his girlfriend?

- **He gave her a ring.**

20

Why did the burglar take a shower?

- **He wanted to make a clean getaway.**

21

Why is a bad joke like a broken pencil?

- **Because it has no point.**

22

Why aren't planets social?

- **They need their space.**

CHAPTER 4
KNOCK-KNOCK JOKES

Knock, knock!
Who's there?
Water.

Water who?
Water you doing in my house?!

Knock, knock!
Who's there?
Hike.

Hike who?
I didn't know you liked Japanese poetry!

3

Knock, knock!

Who's there?
Canoe.

Canoe who?
Canoe come and play? I'm bored!

4

Knock, knock!

Who's there?
Amos.

Amos who?
A mosquito!

5

Knock, knock!

Who's there?
Opportunity.

Opportunity who?
Opportunity doesn't knock twice!

6

Knock, knock!

Who's there?
Doctor.

Doctor who?
Hey, that's my favorite TV show!

7

Knock, knock!

Who's there?
A herd.

A herd who?
A herd you were home, so I came over!

8

Knock, knock!

Who's there?
Donut.

Donut who?
Donut ask me — I just got here!

9

Knock, knock!
Who's there?
Juno.

Juno who?
Juno that I'm out here, right?

10

Knock, knock!
Who's there?
Burglar.

Burglar who?
Burglars don't knock!

Knock, knock!

Who's there?
Police.

Police who?
Police, may I come in?

Knock, knock!

Who's there?
Goat.

Goat who?
Goat to the door and find out.

13

Knock, knock!

Who's there?
Watson.

Watson who?
Watson TV tonight?

14

Knock, knock!

Who's there?
Arya.

Arya who?
Arya ready to go swimming?

15

Knock, knock!

Who's there?
Witches.

Witches who?
Witches the way home?

16

Knock, knock!

Who's there?
Scold.

Scold who?
Scold outside; let me in!

(17)

Knock, knock!

Who's there?
Luke.

Luke who?
Luke through the peephole and find out!

(18)

Knock, knock!

Who's there?
Gorilla.

Gorilla who?
Gorilla me a burger, please. I'm hungry.

19

Knock, knock!

Who's there?
Howard.

Howard who?
Howard I know?

20

Knock, knock!

Who's there?
Al.

Al who?
Al come back later!

21

Knock, knock!
Who's there?
Obama.

Obama who?
O-ba-ma-self!

22

Knock, knock!
Who's there?
Dozen.

Dozen who?
Dozen anyone want to let me in?

1

Why can't Simba be trusted?

- **Because he's a lyin' king.**

2

Why are celebrities so cool?

- **They have a lot of fans.**

What do mothers dress up as on Halloween?

- **Mummies!**

Who made Santa upset?

- **Rude-olf.**

5

What do elves listen to as they prepare gifts?

- **Wrap music.**

6

Why is the skeleton feeling blue?

- **He wants some body to love.**

Why are skeletons easy going?

- **Nothing gets under their skin.**

What birthday should you celebrate by going camping?

- **Your tent-h birthday!**

9

What kind of tree fits in your hand?

- A palm tree.

10

What did the dad chimney say to the little chimney?

- You're too young to smoke!

11

How do we know that the ocean is friendly?

- It waves!

12

What are the strongest days of the week?

- Saturday and Sunday. The rest are weak days.

13

Why can't you ever tell a joke around glass?

- **It could crack up.**

14

What letters are not in the alphabet?

- **The ones in the mail.**

Why can't pirates play cards?

- **They are always on the deck!**

What do you call a man with no body and no nose?

- **Nobody knows!**

What do you call a sleeping tissue?
- **A nap-kin.**

Where would an elephant store its belongings?
- **Mini-soda.**

Why did the phone need its glasses?

- It lost its contacts.

Why was the sun advised to read?

- To grow brighter.

FINAL WORDS

Thanks for reading my book.

I spent years travelling the world looking the best jokes for 12-year-old kids — and nothing makes me happier than knowing that great kids like you are reading them.

But you are not finished yet.

At the start of this book, I said these jokes get funnier the more times you share them — and now it is time to share them.

So, take a deep breath and head back to the start of this book.

Turn the pages and write down your favorite jokes so you can share them with your friends and family — after all, the only thing better than hearing a funny joke is telling a funny joke.

What are you waiting for — head back to the start and get ready to laugh time and time again.

www.ingramcontent.com/pod-product-compliance
Lightning Source LLC
Chambersburg PA
CBHW071408070526
44578CB00002B/516